Indian
COOKING

A culinary journey through India

Indian cooking is among the best in the world.
It combines aromatic herbs and spices with exotic
fruits and tender meat or poultry in a colourful and
utterly mouth-watering way. Whatever you like best
– meat or vegetarian dishes, fiery hot or mildly
spiced – with this book you can enjoy the
specialities of this fascinating country.

Enjoy this unique culinary journey with a
good appetite!

AURA

CONTENTS

The regions

Imagine a vast country populated by a hundred different nationalities, all speaking different languages. Then give each of these its own measure of cultural and regional influences, let centuries pass and you will eventually find a wealth of cuisines, each a little different and all of them truly exotic. Hardly any other country in the world can offer such a wide range of dishes or promise you such a fascinating culinary adventure as India. The immense variety of ingredients and even methods of cooking in Indian cuisine results, to a considerable extent, from the wide variations in climate and topography in the sub-continent, as well as from cultural and religious differences.

The North

A lot of wheat and millet are grown here, so people eat plenty of bread. Lamb, poultry, yogurt, ghee and spices dominate the kitchen. Mogul influence is apparent in the creamy, quite mildly spiced dishes. Both nuts and saffron are used to add interest.

The West

The traditional fare of western India is light and there is a large choice of fish and seafood. The Kerala coast is well known for its various fish curries and prawn dishes. A speciality is lamb or chicken with spiced lentils. The cuisine of west India has also incorporated the largest number of foreign ingredients.

The East

Fish also plays an important part in Bengali cooking in the East. The region has a plentiful supply of seafood from the Ganges Delta and the Bay of Bengal. It is famous for a fish curry flavoured with yogurt, turmeric and ginger. Mustard oil is also characteristic of eastern Indian cooking.

The South

Fish, rice, coconut, vegetables, chillies and cereals, as well as countless aromatic herbs and spices, are just some of the ingredients that are used so abundantly in southern Indian cookery. Specialities are Coconut chutney (recipe on page 54) and Masala dosa (recipe on page 18).

Chillies play an important part in Indian cooking.
After the harvest they are spread out to dry and constantly turned over.

Eating in India

As a rule, Indian cooks do not serve just a single dish at a meal, but offer a choice of various foods. These are served together on a *thali*, a round tray made of silver, brass or stainless steel. Little bowls containing the different dishes are arranged on it. It is traditional to eat with the fingers of the right hand. An Indian meal can be composed of many different dishes and may be wholly vegetarian or include meat, fish or poultry. Even so, vegetables play an important role. Plain, boiled rice or a more elaborate rice dish or one of several kinds of Indian bread – sometimes both – is usually served as an accompaniment. Here is an example of each kind of meal.

Thalis are not just used as serving trays; the different dishes may be eaten directly off them, usually using the fingers of the right hand.

Non-vegetarian thali

- Red lentils with fresh coriander (Masoor dhal, recipe on page 12)
- Potato and cauliflower curry (Alu gobi, recipe on page 22)
- Chicken in almond sauce (Murg man pasand, recipe on page 36)
- Tomato chutney (Tamatar chatni, recipe on page 54)
- Mango dessert (Malai am, recipe on page 56)
- Served with rice

Vegetarian thali

- Aubergine fritters (Pakoras, recipe on page 16) with mint sauce (Dahi poodina, recipe on page 50)
- Puris (Puri, recipe on page 44)
- Split chick peas with coconut (Chana dhal, recipe on page 12)

- Braised spinach with onions (Mughlai sag, recipe on page 22)
- Aubergines in mustard sauce (Baigan kari, recipe on page 26)
- Mango chutney (Am-chatni, recipe on page 52)
- Sweet lassi (Mithi lassi, recipe on page 60)
- Served with rice

At the end of an Indian meal it is customary to chew *pan*. This is a mixture of different spices and betel nuts wrapped in a leaf.

Indian cookery and health

In countries all over the world we eat to satisfy our appetites and to keep our bodies strong and healthy. Like everyone else, people in India eat to survive, but they also think about food in terms of its giving their bodies a physical and spiritual balance. This harmony is best achieved by the careful choice of spices in the preparation of meals and through regular fasting. In India's traditional Ayurvedic medicine, all spices and herbs are ascribed particular healing or preventative properties. It is thought, for example, that pepper is good for treating digestive upsets, turmeric can be used both internally and externally for a number of skin disorders, ginger is considered good for treating colds and liver problems and cloves are thought to strengthen the heart.

This is a collection of typical Indian cooking utensils. Anticlockwise from top left: a chapati pan, sil and batta, karahi or Balti pan, coconut grater and a sieve with a selection of different meshes.

Indian cooking utensils

Generally speaking, you need only the ordinary equipment and utensils found in any western kitchen, such as saucepans, frying pans and chopping boards, for preparing most Indian dishes. An electric blender or food processor can take the place of the traditional grinding stone for pulverizing spices. Smaller quantities of spices and nuts may be ground in an electric coffee grinder kept specially for this purpose and, of course, by hand with a pestle in a mortar. The specialist Indian cooking utensils described below can be found in many Asian shops.

Chalni or charni is a round, fairly flat, fine sieve made of wood or metal. It is used to sieve flour.

Hamal-dista is a mortar for grinding or pounding dry spices. Indian mortars are made of heavy stone or cast iron.

Karahi or Balti pan is a kind of Indian wok. It is a round, deep, curved-bottomed pan, usually made of cast iron. Karahis are available in various sizes. It is especially useful and healthy for frying because its curved shape means that less fat is needed than in a conventional pan. A new karahi should be seasoned before

it is used for the first time. After that, it needs only to be washed in warm water.

Narial kas is a coconut grater made of rotating sharp, curved serrated blades.

Sil and batta are for grinding spices. A sil is a flat stone about 10 cm/ 4 inches thick and a batta is a stone roller used to grind the spices. Whole spices are softened in water, then ground several times to a fine powder.

Tawa is also a cast iron pan, but it is only gently curved. It is ideal for making round flat bread (chapati).

Special ingredients

Spices

Often in Indian cooking, more than thirty spices are assembled, rather like paint on an artist's palette. The knack of using spices lies not only in choosing a single spice and grinding, toasting or frying it in hot fat to achieve different tastes, but also in combining a range of spices. This is how Indian cooking acquires the many delicious aromas that make it so special.

Aniseed

(Mithi sounf)
This is mainly used after meals in India to aid digestion. It has a delicate flavour, rather like liquorice

Asafoetida

(Hing)
This spice (also called devil's dirt because of its powerful smell) is obtain from the root of the *Ferula asafoetida*. It is said to be effective for curing flatulence, stomach cramps and colic. For this reason and because its smell and taste are so powerful, it is only used in small quantities. Always store it in a completely airtight jar to prevents its smell spreading to other ingredients in the kitchen

Fenugreek

(Methi)
The light brown seeds are flat and extremely pungent. They are used in various curry recipes, especially in Sri Lanka. The seeds must be lightly roasted before grinding. Both seeds and the fresh leaves can be used.

Chilli

(Mirch)
There are many kinds of chilli, which range from quite mild to fiery hot. If you do not like your food too spicy, remove some or all the seeds from both fresh and dried chillies. It is sensible to wear rubber gloves when handling chillies and always wash your hands afterwards, avoiding touching your face or eyes. As a general rule, dark green chillies tend to be hotter than pale green, and red chillies, the ripest, are usually milder still. Traditional Indian cookery always uses red chillies but, nowadays, green chillies have become an integral part of Indian cuisine. Dried chillies, which may be used whole or crushed, are extremely fiery and should be used with extreme care.

Curry

The word curry is an English derivation from the Tamil word *kari*, meaning spicy sauce. In India, curry is not a ready-made powder, but a mixture of various spices, such as turmeric, coriander, cumin and many more. Roasted, ground fenugreek is the spice that gives curry its characteristic aroma.

Curry leaves

(Kari pata)
These leaves grow mainly on trees in the south of India and acquired their name from the fact that when they are crushed they smell like a curry mixture. They look very similar to bay leaves. Fresh leaves may be difficult to obtain. If you do see any, however, buy them because they freeze well. Dried curry leaves can be bought in many Asian shops.

Fennel seeds

(Sounf)
These are used in India not only as a flavouring in certain dishes, particularly curries, but also as an important aid in folk medicine. They are useful, among other things, for treating flatulence and are a component in cough syrup. The sweet-tasting seeds are also chewed after meals to aid digestion and freshen the breath.

Five-spice mixture

(Panch foron)
This consists of fenugreek, fennel, cumin, mustard and onion seeds. The spice mixture is fried in hot oil and then used in a variety of vegetable dishes and chutneys. Be careful when you shop for it that you really get the Indian and not the Chinese five-spice mixture, which is completely different.

Garam masala

This is a flavouring mixture of various roasted and ground spices. There is no standard version, as the ingredients differ from region to region and even from cook to cook. Garam masala is usually added towards the end of the cooking time. It is easy to prepare a typical mixture yourself. Dry-fry 15 ml/1 tablespoon coriander seeds, 15 ml/1 tablespoon cumin seeds, 5 ml/1 teaspoon black peppercorns, 2.5 ml/½ teaspoon cardamom pods and 2.5 ml/½ teaspoon cloves, together with 1 cinnamon stick (about 5 cm/2 inches long) in a medium-hot frying pan or karahi, stirring constantly. Set aside to cool and then crush in an electric coffee grinder. Store the mixture in a dark glass, screw-top jar.

Ginger
(Adrak)
Fresh root ginger is peeled and finely grated, chopped or crushed in a mortar with a pestle. Ginger is said to stimulate the appetite, to be anti-inflammatory, to ease coughing and prevent colds.

Cloves
(Loung)
These are the dried buds of the clove tree. Roasted ground cloves are nearly always a component of the spice mixture in garam masala.

Green cardamom
(Choti elaichi)
This is the second most expensive spice in the world after saffron. It is native to India and is said to be an effective medicine in many illnesses. It is used to flavour many savoury and sweet dishes and is also chewed after meals to freshen the breath.

1. paprika 2. aniseed 3. chilli powder
4. garam masala 5. ginger 6. turmeric
7. black and white pepper 8. Five-spice
mixture 9. asafoetida 10. mint
11. fresh chillies 12. mace 13. nutmeg
14. fenugreek 15. cinnamon bark
16. curry leaves 17. curry powder
18. cloves 19. cumin seeds 20. black
cumin seeds 21. fennel seeds
22. coriander seeds 23. black mustard
seeds 24. white poppy seeds 25. ajowan
26. green cardamom 27. onion seeds
28. saffron

Coriander
(Dhania)
Coriander grows almost everywhere in the world. The seeds, stalks and leaves are all used in Indian cooking. Ground coriander, a light brown powder, is a component in nearly every curry mixture. The seeds have a strong aroma and slightly lemon taste.

Cumin
(Jeera)
These brownish seeds are used for nearly all dishes in India. Cumin aids digestion and stimulates the appetite. Black cumin seeds (kala jeera) are smaller than brown and have a slightly bitter taste.

Turmeric
(Haldi)
Bright yellow in colour, turmeric is an important component of curry powder, more for its colouring than its flavour. In India, the fresh root is usually used, but this may be difficult to obtain. If you are using fresh turmeric, protect your hands from staining by wearing rubber gloves. Dry turmeric is readily available. In Indian medicine turmeric is used as a diuretic, to help stomach complaints and for treating skin diseases.

Bay leaves
(Tedschpata)
Both fresh and dried bay leaves are readily available. They are used in nearly all Indian dishes.

Mint
(Poodina)
It is used fresh as a garnish and also in chutney, mint sauce and drinks. If you are unable to get fresh mint, you can substitute

bottled mint that has been shredded and preserved in salt and vinegar. Store in the refrigerator after it has been opened. Indian mint has a stronger aroma than Western varieties.

Poppy seeds (white)
(Khas-khas)
These are usually roasted before they are ground and used to bind and thicken sauces.

Mace
(Javantri)
Mace is the outer covering of the nutmeg. When the fruit is ripe, it splits into a brown nut and a bright red membrane. The membrane is removed, dried in the sun and acquires an orange-red colour.

Nutmeg
(Jaibal)
This is the kernel of the fruit of the tropical nutmeg tree. This spice is used both in sweet and hot dishes. As the aroma is strong, it is best to buy whole nutmegs and grate freshly as required.

Paprika
(Degi mirch)
Indian paprika is quite mild and is comparable to the sweet paprika used in European cooking. In India it is used mainly for its beautiful red colour.

Pepper, black
(Kali-mirch)
This stimulates the appetite and is also used in Indian medicine for its aromatic oils. Both ground pepper and whole peppercorns are used.

Saffron

(Kesar)

This comes from the stigmas of a type of crocus. About 100,000 flowers are needed to produce 1 kg/2¼ lb of saffron. The stigmas have to be pulled out by hand, making saffron the most expensive spice in the world. However, only small quantities are required. It is available in both strands and powdered form. In Indian cooking it is used for its yellow colour and its aroma in rice dishes, for flavouring sweets and in baking.

Mustard seeds, black

(Sarson)

These are noticeably sharper than yellow ones. The seeds are also used for their oil in pickling and for cooking vegetables and fish. You can buy mustard oil in Indian shops. The oil from chemists is too strong for culinary use.

Ajowan

(Ajwain)

These greenish-brown seeds contain thyme oil and smell like thyme when they are crushed. They are used for vegetable dishes and for making certain kinds of bread. If you have difficulty obtaining ajowan seeds – also called bishop's weed – you can successfully substitute thyme.

Cinnamon bark

(Dalchini)

Cinnamon has a sweet, very aromatic flavour and is one of earliest know spices. The bark is dark brown and comes in pieces about 5–10 cm/2–4 inches long. These taste stronger than cinnamon sticks, which are actually pieces of the inner bark. You can buy cinnamon bark in Asian shops. Cinnamon is also available ready ground, but this has less flavour.

Onion seeds

(Kalonji)

These small, black drop-shaped seeds are used in a variety of pickles and also in vegetable and fish curries. They may be scattered over Indian bread.

Pulses

(Dhal)

Split lentils, beans and chick peas are called dhal. (Whole pulses are known as gram.) They are important protein-providers in India, particularly in vegetarian diets. They are highly nutritious and also inexpensive. Because they do not have a very strong flavour, they are extremely versatile, going well with Indian spices. There are about 50 different kinds. Dhal is invariably served as an accompaniment to a main dish and eaten with rice or chapatis.

Chana dhal

These are similar to yellow split peas. They grow in northern India. They can also be used whole, but then the dish is not so creamy.

Masoor dhal

These split red lentils have a relatively short cooking time and a pleasantly mild aroma. Cooking turns them to a pale yellow colour.

Pulses play an important part in Indian cooking: 1. chana dhal 2. masoor dhal 3. moong dhal 4. urid dhal 5. toor dhal.

Other ingredients for Indian cooking are available from Asian shops: 1. papadams 2. besan 3. chapati or ata flour 4. mango pulp 5. ghee.

Moong dhal

These are split mung beans. The dishes made from these are particularly easy to digest and are also simple to prepare.

Toor dhal

These are brownish lentils that are coated with a thin layer of oil. They are also called arahar lentils or arahar dhal.

Urid dhal

These are white split lentils (they are known as black gram when the black hull is retained). They are used mainly in southern Indian cooking. Urid dhal is slightly drier in texture than most other lentils and tends to take a rather longer time to cook.

Other special ingredients

Besan

This is a chick-pea flour from which, for example, batter may be made.

Ata

This special mixture of wheat and wholemeal flour is used for making chapatis (recipe on page 44) and other breads. It is also known as chapati flour.

Ghee

This Indian clarified butter can be bought in Asian shops or you can prepare it yourself. For 750 g/1 lb 10 oz ghee, melt 1 kg/2¼ lb unsalted butter in a large saucepan over a low heat. Lower the temperature and simmer for 30–40 minutes. As soon as the milky part becomes yellow and the ghee is quite clear, strain through clean muslin into another jar and leave to cool. It will keep for months. Many modern Indian cooks prefer vegetable ghee, as it is lower in unsaturated fats.

Mango pulp

This comes from pulped, slightly sweetened Alphonso mangoes, which have a particularly fine fragrance. It can be bought in cans.

Papadam

These are thin, dried-lentil, crisp 'biscuits', which often also include a variety of spices. They may be quickly fried or baked.

Split chick peas with coconut

CHANA DHAL

Speciality of southern India

Serves 4
200 g/7 oz chana dhal
500 ml/17 fl oz water
30 ml/2 tablespoons ghee
(clarified butter)
5 ml/1 teaspoon cumin seeds
2 bay leaves
2 fresh chillies
5 ml/1 teaspoon ground turmeric
5 ml/1 teaspoon sweet paprika
2.5 ml/½ teaspoon sugar
75 g/3 oz grated fresh coconut
salt

Approximately per portion:
1500 kj/360 kcal
11 g protein
16 g fat
43 g carbohydrate

● Approximate preparation
time: 40 minutes

---

1. Put the chana dhal and water in a saucepan and bring to the boil over a moderate heat. Lower the heat, cover and cook slowly over a low heat for about 25 minutes.

2. Melt the ghee in another saucepan over a medium heat. Add the cumin seeds, bay leaves, whole fresh chillies, turmeric, sweet paprika, sugar and grated coconut. Season with salt to taste and cook for about 3 minutes, stirring constantly.

3. Add the spice mixture to the dhal, stir well to mix and serve.

Red lentils with fresh coriander

MASOOR DHAL

Easy to prepare

Serves 4
175 g/6 oz masoor dhal
500 ml/17 fl oz water
2.5 ml/½ teaspoon grated fresh
root ginger
5 ml/1 teaspoon ground turmeric
salt
30 ml/2 tablespoons ghee
(clarified butter)
5 ml/1 teaspoon cumin seeds
5 ml/1 teaspoon ground coriander
pinch asafoetida
1.5 ml/¼ teaspoon chilli powder
30 ml/2 tablespoons chopped
fresh coriander

Approximately per portion:
940 kj/220 kcal
10 g protein
11 g fat
23 g carbohydrate

● Approximate preparation
time: 20 minutes

---

1. Put the masoor dhal and water in a saucepan and bring to the boil. Add the ginger, together with the turmeric and season with salt to taste. Lower the heat, cover the pan and cook the lentils over a medium heat for approximately 10 minutes. Then remove the pan from the heat and set aside.

2. Melt the ghee in a small saucepan over a medium heat. Add the cumin, ground coriander, asafoetida and chilli powder and cook for about 1 minute, stirring constantly. Add the spice mixture to the dhal and mix thoroughly.

3. Transfer the dhal to a warm serving dish, sprinkle over the chopped coriander and serve.

Variation
Instead of fresh coriander you can use flat leaf parsley.

Above: Red lentils with fresh coriander
Below: Split chick peas with coconut

Moong dhal

MOONG DHAL

Easy to prepare

Serves 4
1 onion
4 cm/1½ inch piece of fresh
    root ginger
2 garlic cloves
30 ml/2 tablespoons ghee
    (clarified butter)
2.5 ml/½ teaspoon ground turmeric
5 ml/1 teaspoon ground cumin
250 g/9 oz moong dhal
750 ml/1¼ pints water
salt
2.5 ml/½ teaspoon garam masala
Boiled basmati rice or Chapatis,
    to serve

Approximately per portion:
1600 kj/380 kcal
23 g protein
25 g fat
17 g carbohydrate

● Approximate preparation
   time: 40 minutes

---

1. Finely chop the onion. Grate
the ginger. Grate, crush or finely
chop the garlic.

2. Melt the ghee in a medium
saucepan. Add the onion, garlic
and ginger and cook over a
medium heat, stirring constantly,
until the onion is golden brown.
Add the turmeric and cumin and
cook, stirring constantly, for a
further 2 minutes.

3. Add the moong dhal and cook
for 2 minutes. Then add the water
and salt to taste.

4. Bring the mixture to the boil,
lower the heat, cover and cook for
about 25 minutes, until the lentils
are soft. Finally sprinkle the garam
masala over the mixture. Serve
warm with Boiled basmati rice
(recipe on page 42) or Chapatis
(recipe on page 44).

Toor dhal soup

TOOR DHAL

For guests

Toor dhal are special lentils coated
with a layer of oil, which dissolves
when they are cooked.

Serves 4
1 litre/1¾ pints water
250 g/9 oz toor dhal
2.5 ml/½ teaspoon ground turmeric
2.5 ml/½ teaspoon chilli powder
5 ml/1 teaspoon paprika
30 ml/2 tablespoons ghee
    (clarified butter)
5 ml/1 teaspoon cumin seeds
1 fresh chilli
3 bay leaves
5 ml/1 teaspoon sugar
salt
5 ml/1 teaspoon garam masala
Boiled basmati rice or Chapatis,
    to serve

Approximately per portion:
1200 kj/290 kcal
15 g protein
11 g fat
34 g carbohydrate

● Approximate preparation
   time: 45 minutes

---

1. Bring the water to the boil in a
saucepan. Stir in the toor dhal,
cover and simmer for about
25 minutes over medium heat.
Stir well from time to time.

2. Add the ground turmeric, chilli
powder and paprika and cook the
dhal for a further 10 minutes, until
the lentils are soft. Remove the
pan from the heat and set aside.

3. Melt the ghee in a small
saucepan. Add the cumin seeds,
fresh chilli and bay leaves and cook
for about 1 minute, until the spices
turn light brown. Add the mixture
of cumin, chilli and bay leaves to
the dhal and mix thoroughly.

4. Season with sugar and salt to
taste. Sprinkle the garam masala
over the mixture and serve warm
with Boiled basmati rice (recipe on
page 42) or Chapatis (recipe on
page 44).

Tip

When buying fresh ginger, look
for a plump root that is as
smooth as possible. Soft,
wrinkled ginger roots have been
lying around in the shop for too
long. Store, unpeeled and tightly
wrapped with clear film, in the
refrigerator, where it will keep
for up to six weeks. Peel the
skin thinly with a vegetable
peeler before grating or
chopping finely.

Above: Moong dhal
Below: Toor dhal soup

Aubergine fritters

PAKORAS

For guests

Serves 6
500 g/1 ¼ lb aubergines
250 g/9 oz gram flour
7.5 ml/1½ teaspoons salt
5 ml/1 teaspoon ground cumin
2.5 ml/½ teaspoon chilli powder
5 ml/1 teaspoon ground coriander
5 ml/1 teaspoon sweet paprika
5 ml/1 teaspoon ajowan
5 ml/1 teaspoon onion seeds
30 ml/2 tablespoons lukewarm water
vegetable oil, for deep-frying
Mint sauce or Mango chutney, to serve

Approximately per portion:
1200 kj/290 kcal
9 g protein
18 g fat
23 g carbohydrate

● Approximate preparation
time: 45 minutes

---

1. Cut the aubergines into slices about 5 mm/¼ inch thick.

2. Put the gram flour into a bowl and stir in the salt, cumin, chilli powder, coriander, sweet paprika, ajowan and onion seeds. Gradually add the lukewarm water, beating constantly with a whisk to make a smooth, thick batter.

3. Heat the vegetable oil in a deep-fryer or karahi until a small spoonful of batter dropped in will hiss and rise to the surface immediately.

4. Dip the aubergine slices in the batter and drop into the hot oil, in batches if necessary. Fry the pakoras for a few minutes, until they are golden brown and crisp. Remove from the pan, drain well on kitchen paper and keep warm while you cook the remainder. Serve warm with Mint sauce (recipe on page 50) or Mango chutney (recipe on page 52).

Variation
You can make pakoras with different vegetables: peel 500 g/ 1¼ lb potatoes and cut into 3 mm/ ⅛ inch thick slices; or cut a small cauliflower into florets about 5 cm/ 2 inches in size; or peel 500 g/ 1¼ lb onions and slice into rings about 5 mm/¼ inch thick. Prepare the batter as above.

Vegetable patties

SABZI CHOP

For guests

Serves 4
300 g/11 oz floury potatoes
150 g/5 oz carrots
150 g/5 oz beetroot
125 ml/4 fl oz water
50 g/2 oz white cabbage
2 onions
45 ml/3 tablespoons ghee
*   (clarified butter)*
2.5 ml/½ teaspoon chilli powder
5 ml/1 teaspoon paprika
5 ml/1 teaspoon ground cumin
salt
1 egg
150 g/5 oz breadcrumbs
vegetable oil, for deep-frying

Approximately per portion:
1500 kj/360 kcal
9 g protein
17 g fat
44 g carbohydrate

● Approximate preparation
time: 45 minutes

---

1. Peel and finely chop the potatoes, carrots and beetroot.

2. Put the chopped vegetables and water into a saucepan and bring to the boil. Cover and boil over a medium heat until they are soft. Strain, then mash and set aside.

3. Meanwhile shred the white cabbage and peel and finely chop the onions. Melt the ghee in a saucepan and fry the onions until golden brown. Add the white cabbage and cook for a further 10 minutes over a medium heat.

4. Put all the vegetables into a bowl and mix in the chilli powder, paprika and cumin. Season with salt to taste. Divide the mixture into 12 and, using your hands, form into 12 patties. Set aside to cool.

5. Lightly beat the egg and pour it on to a plate. Put the breadcrumbs on another plate . Dip the patties first into the egg and then into the breadcrumbs to coat thoroughly.

6. Heat the vegetable oil in a deep frying pan or karahi. Fry the patties, in batches if necessary, for 2–4 minutes on each side over a medium heat. Remove with a slotted spoon and drain on kitchen paper. Serve hot.

Above: Vegetable patties
Below: Aubergine fritters

Pancakes with spicy filling

MASALA DOSA

Rather time-consuming

In southern India these pancakes are always freshly prepared. They should be served hot. Masala dosa are served with Coconut chutney (recipe on page 54).

Serves 6
150 g/5 oz rice
150 g/5 g urid dhal
about 300 ml/½ pint water
2 fresh chillies
5 ml/1 teaspoon muscovado sugar
salt
8 medium floury potatoes
3 cm/1¼ inch piece fresh root ginger
45 ml/3 tablespoons grated coconut
about 90 ml/6 tablespoons ghee
  (clarified butter) or vegetable oil
10 ml/2 teaspoons cumin seeds
10 ml/2 teaspoons black
  mustard seeds
5 ml/1 teaspoon ground turmeric
30 ml/2 tablespoons chopped fresh
  coriander leaves
fresh coriander leaves, to garnish
Coconut chutney, to serve

Approximately per portion:
1800 kj/430 kcal
9 g protein
22 g fat
47 g carbohydrate

● Soaking time: 1½ days

● Approximate preparation time: about 2 hours

---

1. Put the rice in a bowl, add sufficient cold water to cover and set aside for 8 hours to soak. Put the urid dhal in another bowl, add sufficient water to cover and set aside for 8 hours to soak. Drain the rice well and grind in a food processor. Set aside. Drain the urid dhal well and grind in a food processor. Add the ground dhal to the rice and mix in about 300 ml/ ½ pint water to make a thin batter.

2. Seed and finely chop 1 fresh chilli. Add it to the rice and dhal mixture, together with the sugar and 2.5 ml/½ teaspoon salt and mix well. Cover the bowl with a clean cloth and set aside to stand for 24 hours in a warm place.

3. Next day prepare the filling. Cook the potatoes in their skins in a little boiling water for about 20 minutes, until just tender. Peel and mash coarsely with a potato masher and set aside. Finely chop the ginger. Seed and finely chop the remaining chilli. Mix together the chopped ginger, chopped chilli and the grated coconut to make a fairly thick paste, adding a little water if necessary.

4. Melt the ghee or heat the vegetable oil in a medium saucepan. Stir-fry the cumin seeds and mustard seeds. When the mustard seeds begin to pop, add the chilli, ginger and coconut mixture and cook for about 1 minute. Then add the turmeric, potatoes and chopped coriander leaves and season to taste with salt. Cook for about 5 minutes, stirring constantly. Remove the pan from the heat, cover and set aside.

5. Beat the batter again. It should be a thick liquid, but if it is too thick, add a little water. Preheat a large frying pan over a medium heat. Test by sprinkling a few drops of water into the pan. If they sizzle, the pan is hot enough.

6. Put 5 ml/1 teaspoon ghee or oil into the pan. Pour about 250 ml/ 8 fl oz of the batter quickly and evenly into the pan, using a spoon to spread it thinly over the base. (The pancake should be about 20 cm/8 inches in diameter.) Fry the pancake for about 2 minutes, until golden brown. Using a spatula, turn it over and fry for a further 2 minutes. Slide the pancake out on to a plate and keep warm. Fry all the pancakes in the same way, adding a little ghee or vegetable oil as required. Stack the cooked pancakes on the plate, interleaved with greaseproof paper and keep them warm and moist.

7. When all the pancakes are ready, spoon one-sixth of the potato filling over half of 1 pancake and fold over in the middle. Alternatively, spread the filling down the centre of the pancake and fold each side inwards to cover it. Repeat with the remaining filling and pancakes. Then fry the filled dosas again on each side for about 30 seconds. Garnish with fresh coriander leaves and serve warm with Coconut chutney (recipe on page 54).

Spicy pancakes are filled before being folded over and quickly fried once more.

Vegetable samosas

SAMOSA

Famous recipe

Makes 16 samosas
For the filling:
400 g/14 oz floury potatoes
400 g/14 oz cauliflower
3 cm/1¼ inch piece fresh root ginger
45 ml/3 tablespoons ghee
2.5 ml/½ teaspoon cumin seeds
2.5 ml/½ teaspoon black cumin
* seeds (kala jeera)*
1.5 ml/¼ teaspoon chilli powder
5 ml/1 teaspoon ground coriander
5 ml/1 teaspoon sweet paprika
90 g/3½ oz frozen peas
5 ml/1 teaspoon garam masala
5 ml/1 teaspoon salt

For the dough:
300 g/11 oz flour
60 ml/4 tablespoons ghee
* (clarified butter) or vegetable oil*
5 ml/1 teaspoon salt
175 ml/6 fl oz water
vegetable oil, for deep-frying

Approximately per portion:
1000 kj/240 kcal
3 g protein
18 g fat
20 g carbohydrate

● Approximate preparation
  time: 1½ hours

1. First make the filling. Cut the potatoes into 1 cm/½ inch cubes. Cut the cauliflower into small florets. Grate the ginger.

2. Melt the ghee in a saucepan. Add both kinds of cumin seeds and stir-fry over a medium heat for about 1 minute. Stir in the chilli powder, ground coriander and paprika. Add the ginger, potatoes, cauliflower and peas. Cook, stirring occasionally, for about 5 minutes.

3. Reduce the heat, cover the pan and cook for about 10 minutes, until the vegetables are quite soft. Add a little water if the mixture seems to be becoming too dry or looks as if it might be about to burn. Sprinkle over the garam masala and salt and briefly stir. Transfer the vegetable mixture to a bowl and leave to cool.

4. To make the dough, put the flour, ghee or vegetable oil, salt and water into a bowl. Knead the mixture for about 15 minutes, until the dough is firm and smooth. Cover the bowl with a damp cloth and set aside to rest for about 10 minutes.

5. Divide the dough into 8 pieces and roll each into a ball with the palms of your hands. On an oiled wooden board roll out each ball into a flat circle about 13 cm/ 5 inches in diameter. Cut each dough circle in half.

Tip

Samosas are the most popular Indian snack. For a change you can make the filling with other vegetables or with minced meat. They are good with pickles, chutneys (recipes on pages 52 and 54) or Mint sauce (recipe on page 50).

6. Fold each semi-circle to form a bag. Press the longer side of each bag firmly together with moistened fingers to seal. Put 10 ml/ 2 teaspoons of the prepared filling into a dough bag and seal the edges with moistened fingers. Prepare the other samosas in the same way.

7. Heat the oil in a large pan or karahi. Add 3 or 4 samosas and fry until golden.

8. Remove the samosas with a slotted spoon and drain well on kitchen paper. Keep warm while you fry the remainder in the same way. Serve the samosas warm as a starter or snack.

Braised spinach with onions

MUGHLAI SAG

Quick to make

Serves 4
2 onions
3 cm/1¼ inch piece fresh root ginger
2 garlic cloves
3 tablespoons ghee (clarified butter)
    or vegetable oil
1.5 ml/¼ teaspoon chilli powder
5 ml/1 teaspoon ground cumin
2.5 ml/½ teaspoon ground turmeric
5 ml/1 teaspoon ground coriander
600 g/1 lb 5 oz frozen
    spinach, thawed
salt
120 ml/4 fl oz double cream
Chapatis, to serve

Approximately per portion:
1110 kj/270 kcal
5 g protein
20 g fat
4 g carbohydrate

● Approximate preparation
   time: 25 minutes

---

1. Thinly slice the onions, grate the ginger and crush the garlic.

2. Melt the ghee or heat the oil in a karahi or frying pan. Fry the onions, ginger and garlic over a medium heat until golden brown.

3. Add the chilli powder, cumin, turmeric and coriander and fry for about 1 minute. Add the spinach and salt to taste. Cover and simmer for about 15 minutes.

4. Stir in the cream and heat through, but do not allow it to boil. Serve the spinach with Chapatis (recipe on pages 44).

Potato and cauliflower curry

ALU GOBI

Easy to make

Serves 4
350 g/12 oz cauliflower
350 g/12 oz waxy potatoes
2 medium onions
2 fresh chillies
3 cm/1¼ inch piece fresh root ginger
2 tomatoes
90 ml/6 tablespoons vegetable oil
5 ml/1 teaspoon five-spice mixture
    (panch foron)
7.5 ml/1½ teaspoons ground
    turmeric
7.5 ml/1½ teaspoons ground cumin
10 ml/2 teaspoons sweet paprika
1.5 ml/¼ teaspoon chilli powder
200 g/7 oz frozen peas
45 ml/3 tablespoons full-fat yogurt
salt
250 ml/8 fl oz water
5 ml/1 teaspoon garam masala
Boiled basmati rice or Naan,
    to serve

Approximately per portion:
1500 kj/360 kcal
8 g protein
26 g fat
24 g carbohydrate

● Approximate preparation
   time: 50 minutes

---

1. Divide the cauliflower into florets about 5 cm/2 inches long. Peel the potatoes and cut into 3 cm/1¼ inch dice. Finely chop the onions. Seed and finely chop the fresh chillies. Grate the ginger. Cut the tomatoes into quarters.

2. Heat the oil in a karahi or heavy-based frying pan. Add the five-spice mixture and the onions. Fry over medium heat, stirring constantly, until the onions are golden brown.

3. Add the potatoes, cauliflower and fresh chillies to the pan and fry for a further 3 minutes, stirring constantly. Add the turmeric, cumin, sweet paprika, chilli powder and ginger and fry for a further 3–4 minutes.

4. Gradually stir in the tomatoes, peas and yogurt. Add the water and salt to taste. Simmer the vegetable mixture over a medium heat for about 20 minutes, stirring occasionally, until the cauliflower and potatoes are soft.

5. Transfer the mixture to a serving dish and sprinkle over the garam masala. Serve the potato and cauliflower curry with Boiled basmati rice (recipe on page 42) or Naan (recipe on page 46).

Above: Braised spinach with onions
Below: Potato and cauliflower curry

Egg biriyani

ANDA BIRIYANI
From northern India

Serves 6
400 g/14 oz basmati rice
3 onions
6 tablespoons ghee (clarified butter)
500 ml/17 fl oz water
350 g/12 oz cauliflower
250 g/9 oz waxy potatoes
2 tomatoes
4 cm/1½ inch piece fresh root ginger
3 cloves
5 cm/2 inch piece cinnamon bark
3 green cardamom pods
2 bay leaves
2.5 ml/½ teaspoon ground turmeric
2.5 ml/½ teaspoon sweet paprika
2.5 ml/½ teaspoon chilli powder
2.5 ml/½ teaspoon ground cumin
200 g/7 oz frozen peas
30 ml/2 tablespoons yogurt
salt
30 ml/2 tablespoons chopped, blanched almonds
30 ml/2 tablespoons currants
3 hard-boiled eggs

Approximately per portion:
2500 kj/600 kcal
15 g protein
29 g fat
67 g carbohydrate

● Approximate preparation time: 2 hours

1. Wash the rice and leave to drain in a sieve for about 30 minutes. Finely chop 1 onion. Heat 45 ml/3 tablespoons of the ghee in a medium saucepan and fry the chopped onion until golden brown. Add the rice and fry for about 3 minutes. Pour in half the water and bring to the boil. Cover and cook for about 10 minutes. It should be only half cooked. Remove the pan from the heat and set aside.

2. Cut the cauliflower into 2 cm/¾ inch florets. Cut the potatoes into 3 cm/1¼ inch cubes. Cut the tomatoes into quarters. Finely chop the remaining onions and grate the ginger.

3. Melt the remaining ghee in a large saucepan. Fry the cloves, cinnamon, cardamom and bay leaves over a medium heat for about 3 minutes, stirring constantly. Gradually stir in the onions, cauliflower and potatoes.

4. Add the turmeric, paprika, chilli powder, cumin, ginger, tomatoes and peas and fry for a further 2 minutes. Stir in the yogurt. Add the remaining water and salt to taste, cover and cook the vegetables for about 5 minutes. They should be only half cooked.

5. Meanwhile, preheat the oven to 200°C/400°F/Gas 6. Rinse an ovenproof casserole with warm water. Spoon half the rice mixture into the base of the casserole, cover with the almonds, currants and vegetable mixture and top with the remaining rice mixture.

6. Cover and cook in the oven for 1 hour. Remove the casserole from the oven and mix well. Shell the eggs and cut into quarters lengthways. Garnish the biriyani with the hard-boiled eggs and serve immediately.

Fried mooli

MOOLI
Good value

Serves 4
1 mooli
45 ml/3 tablespoons vegetable oil
2.5 ml/½ teaspoon onion seeds
1.5 ml/¼ teaspoon ground turmeric
1.5 ml/¼ teaspoon sweet paprika
salt

Approximately per portion:
410 kj/100 kcal
1 g protein
10 g fat
1 g carbohydrate

● Approximate preparation time: 30 minutes

1. Cut the mooli in half lengthways and cut into 3 mm/⅛ inch slices.

2. Heat the oil in a frying pan over a medium heat and stir-fry the onion seeds for about 30 seconds, then add the mooli and stir-fry for a further 3 minutes.

3. Stir in the turmeric, paprika and salt to taste. Cover and cook over a low heat for about 20 minutes, stirring occasionally to prevent burning. Serve hot.

Above: Egg biriyani
Below: Fried mooli

Aubergines in mustard sauce

BAIGAN KARI

Easy to make

Serves 4
400 g/14 oz aubergines
salt
10 ml/2 teaspoons ground turmeric
1 fresh chilli
3 cm/1¼ inch piece fresh root ginger
2 tomatoes
about 45 ml/3 tablespoons
    vegetable oil
75 ml/5 tablespoons mustard oil
2.5 ml/½ teaspoon chilli powder
10 ml/2 teaspoons ground cumin
10 ml/2 teaspoons sweet paprika
45 ml/3 tablespoons full-fat yogurt
200 ml/7 fl oz water
10 ml/2 teaspoons ground black
    mustard seeds

Approximately per portion:
1300 kj/310 kcal
2 g protein
31 g fat
4 g carbohydrate

● Approximate preparation
   time: 45 minutes

---

1. Cut the aubergines into 1 cm/
½ inch slices. Rub the aubergine
slices with 2.5 ml/½ teaspoon salt
and 2.5 ml/½ teaspoon turmeric
and leave to stand for about
10 minutes. Seed and finely chop
the chillies. Grate the ginger. Cut
the tomatoes into quarters.

2. Heat the oil in a heavy-based
frying pan. Lightly fry the aubergine
slices on both sides until golden.

Remove from the pan and drain
thoroughly on kitchen paper. The
aubergines can be fried in batches,
if necessary.

3. Heat the mustard oil in a clean
pan. Add the fresh chilli, the chilli
powder, the remaining turmeric,
the cumin, paprika and ginger and
fry for about 5 minutes over a
medium heat, stirring constantly.
Add the tomatoes and the yogurt
and mix well. Fry the mixture for
about 3 more minutes, until it
forms a brown paste. Stir in the
water and bring to the boil.

4. Add the ground mustard seeds
and aubergines to the pan and
season to taste with salt. Simmer
over a low heat for about
5 minutes. Serve hot.

Okra with coconut milk

BHINDI SABJI

Exquisite

Serves 2–4
500 g/1¼ lb okra
2 medium onions
2 garlic cloves
4 fully ripe tomatoes
3 cm/1¼ inch piece fresh root ginger
45 ml/3 tablespoons ghee
    (clarified butter)
5 ml/1 teaspoon ground cumin
5 ml/1 teaspoon ground coriander
2.5 ml/½ teaspoon ground turmeric
5 ml/1 teaspoon sweet paprika
1.5 ml/¼ teaspoon chilli powder
375 ml/13 fl oz coconut milk
salt
Boiled basmati rice, to serve

**For 4 persons
approximately per portion:**
930 kj/230 kcal
4 g protein
21 g fat
8 g carbohydrate

● Approximate preparation
   time: 55 minutes

---

1. Trim the okra and cut into
pieces about 2 cm/¾ inch long.
Finely chop the onion. Finely chop
the garlic. Cut the tomatoes into
2 cm/¾ inch pieces. Finely chop
the ginger.

2. Melt the ghee in a frying pan or
karahi. Add the onions and fry
until golden brown. Add the garlic
and ginger and fry for about
5 minutes, stirring constantly.

3. Add the cumin, coriander,
turmeric, paprika and chilli powder
and fry, stirring constantly, for
3–4 minutes. Add the okra pieces
and fry, stirring constantly, for a
further 3 minutes.

4. Gradually stir in the tomatoes
and the coconut milk and season
to taste with salt. Bring to the boil,
lower the heat and simmer for
about 25 minutes over a low heat
until the okra is soft. Add water, if
necessary to prevent burning.
Serve with Boiled basmati rice
(recipe on page 42).

Above: Aubergines in mustard sauce
Below: Okra with coconut milk

Rice, lentils and vegetable hotpot

KHITCHURI

For guests

Serves 4–6
½ cauliflower
200 g/7 oz waxy potatoes
2 onions
2 tomatoes
1 fresh chilli
4 tablespoons ghee (clarified butter)
3 bay leaves
5 ml/1 teaspoon ground turmeric
5 ml/1 teaspoon ground cumin
7.5 ml/1½ teaspoon sweet paprika
1.5 ml/¼ teaspoon chilli powder
200 g/7 oz basmati rice
200 g/7 oz masoor dhal
115 g/4 oz frozen peas
salt
1.5 litres/2½ pints water
5 ml/1 teaspoon garam masala
Pakoras, pickles and chutney,
    to serve

**For 6 people approximately
per portion:**
1900 kj/450 kcal
14 g protein
21 g fat
50 g carbohydrate

● Approximate preparation
time: 1 hour

---

1. Cut the cauliflower into florets about 3 cm/1¼ inch long. Cut the potatoes into 3 cm/1¼ inch dice. Finely chop the onions. Cut the tomatoes into quarters. Seed and finely chop the fresh chilli.

2. Melt 45 ml/3 tablespoons of the ghee in a large saucepan and fry the onions until well browned. Add the chopped fresh chilli, bay leaves, turmeric, cumin, paprika and chilli powder and fry over a low heat for about 3 minutes.

3. Gradually stir in the rice, lentils, potatoes, cauliflower, tomatoes and peas.

4. Add salt to taste. Pour in the water and bring to the boil. Lower the heat, cover and simmer, without stirring, for about 25 minutes, until the rice is tender and has absorbed all the liquid.

5. Melt the remaining ghee and pour over the mixture. Transfer to a warm serving dish and sprinkle over the garam masala. Serve with Pakoras (recipe on page 16), pickles and chutney.

Potato curry with poppy seeds

ALU POSTO

Easy to make

Serves 2
500 g/1¼ lb waxy potatoes
2 fresh chillies
2 cm/¾ inch piece fresh root ginger
45 ml/3 tablespoons white
    poppy seeds
75 ml/5 tablespoons mustard oil
5 ml/1 teaspoon ground turmeric
5 ml/1 teaspoon sweet paprika
1.5 ml/¼ teaspoon chilli powder
400 ml/14 fl oz water
salt

Approximately per portion:
2400 kj/570 kcal
8 g protein
44 g fat
39 g carbohydrate

● Approximate preparation
time: 35 minutes

---

1. Cut the potatoes into 2 cm/¾ inch cubes. Seed and finely chop the fresh chillies. Grate the ginger. Grind the white poppy seeds in a coffee grinder or in a mortar with a pestle.

2. Heat the mustard oil in a karahi or heavy-based frying pan over a medium heat. Add the potatoes and fry for about 5 minutes, stirring constantly.

3. Add the fresh chillies, ginger, turmeric, paprika and chilli powder and stir-fry for about 3 minutes, until the spices are dark brown, but not black. Pour in the water, add salt to taste and stir well. Bring to the boil briefly.

4. Scatter in the ground poppy seeds and mix well. Cover and cook over a low heat, stirring occasionally, until the potatoes are soft and cooked through.

Variation
Substitute diced courgettes for half the potatoes.

*Above: Rice, lentils and vegetable hotpot
Below: Potato curry with poppy seeds*

Egg curry

ANDA KARI
For guests

Serve 4
4 hard-boiled eggs
7.5 ml/1½ teaspoon ground turmeric
200 ml/7 fl oz vegetable oil
250 g/9 oz waxy potatoes
4 onions
2 garlic cloves
4 cm/1½ inch piece fresh root ginger
60 ml/4 tablespoons ghee
(clarified butter)
3 green cardamom pods
3 cloves
3 x 5 cm/2 inch pieces
cinnamon bark
2 bay leaves
2.5 ml/½ teaspoon chilli powder
salt
250 ml/8 fl oz water
5 ml/1 teaspoon garam masala

Approximately per portion:
2100 kj/500 kcal
9 g protein
46 g fat
14 g carbohydrate

● Approximate preparation
time: 1 hour

---

1. Shell the eggs, make several cuts in each and sprinkle 1.5 ml/ ¼ teaspoon of the turmeric over them. Heat half the oil in a frying pan, add the eggs and fry them quickly, until lightly coloured. Remove the eggs from the pan and set aside.

2. Cut the potatoes into 3 cm/ 1¼ inch cubes. Sprinkle 1.5 ml/ ¼ teaspoon of the remaining turmeric over them. Heat 30 ml/ 2 tablespoons of the remaining oil in a clean pan and fry the potatoes until golden. Remove from the pan and set aside.

3. Finely chop the onions and garlic. Grate the ginger.

4. Melt the ghee and fry the onions, cardamom, cloves, cinnamon and bay leaves over a medium heat for about 5 minutes. Add the remaining turmeric, the chilli powder and ginger and fry for a further 5 minutes.

5. Add the potatoes, eggs, salt to taste and the water. Cover and simmer for about 20 minutes over a medium heat, until the potatoes are tender.

6. Heat the remaining oil and fry the garam masala and garlic for 2 minutes. Transfer the curry to a serving dish; you can cut the eggs in half if wished. Sprinkle over the garam masala and garlic and serve.

White cabbage with peas

BANDHA GOBI
Easy to make

Serves 4
500 g/1¼ lb white cabbage
250 g/9 oz waxy potatoes
2 tomatoes
45 ml/3 tablespoons ghee
(clarified butter) or
75 ml/5 tablespoons vegetable oil
3 bay leaves
2.5 ml/½ teaspoon cumin seeds
5 ml/1 teaspoon ground turmeric
2.5 ml/½ teaspoon chilli powder
7.5 ml/1½ teaspoons ground cumin
5 ml/1 teaspoon ground coriander
2.5 ml/½ teaspoon sugar
salt
150 g/5 oz frozen peas

Approximately per portion:
990 kj/240 kcal
5 g protein
15 g fat
20 g carbohydrate

● Approximate preparation
time: 50 minutes

---

1. Shred or finely chop the white cabbage. Cut the potatoes into small cubes. Dice the tomatoes.

2. Melt the ghee or heat the oil in a karahi or heavy-based frying pan over a medium heat. Add the bay leaves and the cumin seeds and stir-fry briefly.

3. Add the potatoes and white cabbage and stir-fry for about 3 minutes.

4. Gradually stir in the turmeric, chilli powder, ground cumin, ground coriander, tomatoes, sugar and salt to taste.

5. Cover and cook over a low heat for about 15 minutes. Add the peas, cover and simmer for a further 5 minutes, until the vegetables are soft. Add a little water, if necessary, and stir from time to time to prevent burning. Serve hot.

Above: White cabbage with peas
Below: Egg curry

Red paprika lamb hotpot

ROGAN JOSH

Rather time-consuming

Serves 6
1 kg/2¼ lb boned shoulder of lamb
4 cm/1½ inch piece fresh root ginger
4 garlic cloves
350 ml/12 fl oz water
6 onions
10 tablespoons ghee
 (clarified butter)
8 green cardamom pods
6 cloves
3 bay leaves
8 black peppercorns
2 x 5 cm/2 inch pieces
 cinnamon bark
20 ml/4 teaspoons sweet paprika
2.5 ml/½ teaspoon chilli powder
10 ml/2 teaspoons ground coriander
10 ml/2 teaspoons ground cumin
salt
90 ml/6 tablespoons full-fat yogurt
2.5 ml/½ teaspoon garam masala

Approximately per portion:
3000 kj/710 kcal
32 g protein
64 g fat
6 g carbohydrate

● Approximate preparation
 time: 1¾ hours

1. Trim the lamb and cut it into 2 cm/¾ inch cubes. Put the ginger, garlic and 60 ml/4 tablespoons of the water in a food processor and work to make a purée. Alternatively, pound together in a mortar with a pestle until puréed. Finely chop the onions.

2. Melt the ghee in a karahi or large frying pan. Add the meat and fry, stirring occasionally, until browned on all sides. Remove the meat from the pan and set aside. Add the cardamom, cloves, bay leaves, peppercorns and cinnamon bark to the pan and fry quickly.

3. Add the onions and fry until brown. Add the ginger paste and fry for a further 1 minute. Add the paprika, chilli powder, ground coriander, cumin and salt to taste, then fry for 1 more minute.

4. Return the meat to the pan, stir in the yogurt and heat through for about 5 minutes. Add the remaining water and bring to the boil. Cover and cook over a low heat, stirring occasionally, for about 50 minutes, or until the lamb is cooked through and tender. Sprinkle over the garam masala and serve immediately.

Lamb with spinach

PALAK GOSHT

Easy to make • Exquisite

Serves 4
600 g/1 lb 5 oz boned lamb
600 g/1 lb 5 oz spinach
5 onions
3 cm/1¼ inch piece fresh root ginger
4 garlic cloves
120 ml/8 tablespoons vegetable oil
1.5 ml/¼ teaspoon black
 peppercorns
5 cloves
2 bay leaves
5 green cardamom pods
10 ml/2 teaspoons ground cumin

1.5 ml/¼ teaspoon chilli powder
7.5 ml/1½ teaspoons ground turmeric
10 ml/2 teaspoons sweet paprika
30 ml/2 tablespoons finely chopped
 fresh fenugreek leaves
salt
5 ml/1 teaspoon garam masala
90 ml/6 tablespoons double cream

Approximately per portion:
3000 kj/710 kcal
33 g protein • 61 g fat
9 g carbohydrate

● Approximate preparation
 time: 1½ hours

1. Cut the meat into 2 cm/¾ inch cubes. Finely chop the spinach and onions. Grate the ginger and garlic.

2. Heat the oil in a karahi or large frying pan over a medium heat. Add the peppercorns, cloves, bay leaves and cardamom pods and stir-fry for about 1 minute. Add the onions and fry until they are well browned. Add the garlic and the ginger and stir-fry together for a further 2 minutes.

3. Add the lamb and fry for about 3 minutes. Add the cumin, chilli powder, turmeric, paprika and fenugreek and stir-fry for a further 2 minutes. Add the spinach and salt to taste and cook, stirring, until the spinach breaks down.

4. Cover and cook over a low heat for about 50 minutes, until the meat is tender. Add the garam masala and cream and simmer for a further 5 minutes. Serve hot.

Above: Lamb with spinach
Below: Red paprika lamb hotpot

Lamb Vindaloo

VINDALOO
Famous dish

Serves 6
For the Vindaloo paste:
2.5 ml/½ teaspoon cardamom seeds
2 dried chillies
10 ml/2 teaspoons cumin seeds
5 ml/1 teaspoon black peppercorns
5 ml/1 teaspoon black
   mustard seeds
2 x 5 cm/2 inch pieces
   cinnamon bark
5 ml/1 teaspoon fenugreek seeds
60 ml/4 tablespoons white
   wine vinegar
10 ml/2 teaspoons brown sugar
30 ml/2 tablespoons water
5 ml/1 teaspoon salt

For the meat:
1 kg/2¼ lb boned leg of lamb
4 onions • 6 garlic cloves
4 cm/1½ inch piece fresh root ginger
350 ml/12 fl oz water
90 ml/6 tablespoons ghee
   (clarified butter) or vegetable oil
5 ml/1 teaspoon ground coriander
10 ml/2 teaspoons ground turmeric
10 ml/2 teaspoons sweet paprika
5 ml/1 teaspoon chilli powder
30 ml/2 tablespoons tomato paste
salt
Boiled basmati rice, to serve

> **Approximately per portion:**
> 2700 kj/640 kcal
> 31 g protein
> 55 g fat
> 6 g carbohydrate
>
> ● Approximate preparation
>   time: 2 hours

1. For the Vindaloo paste, grind together the cardamom seeds, dried chilli, cumin, peppercorns, mustard seeds, cinnamon bark and fenugreek in a food processor, an electric coffee grinder or in a mortar with a pestle. Transfer the spice mixture to a bowl. Add the white wine vinegar, brown sugar, water and salt, mix thoroughly and set aside.

2. Cut the meat into 2 cm/¾ inch cubes. Chop the onions and purée in a food processor or electric blender. Chop the garlic and ginger and purée in a food processor or electric blender, together with 60 ml/4 tablespoons of the water.

3. Heat 75 ml/5 tablespoons of the ghee or oil in a saucepan. Fry the onions over a medium heat, stirring, until well browned. Stir in the Vindaloo paste. Remove the pan from the heat.

4. Heat the remaining ghee or oil in a frying pan. Add the meat cubes in batches, and fry until browned on all sides. Remove from the pan and set aside while you fry the remaining batches.

5. Add the ginger and garlic paste to the pan and stir-fry for about 1 minute over a medium heat. Add the coriander, turmeric, paprika,

---

chilli powder and tomato paste and stir-fry for a further 1 minute.

6. Stir in the meat and onion mixture and season with salt to taste. Add the remaining water and bring to the boil. Cover and cook over a low heat, stirring occasionally, for about 45 minutes, until the lamb is tender. Serve with Boiled basmati rice (recipe on page 42).

Tip
Vindaloo dishes are usually very hot. You can reduce the amount of chilli powder according to taste.

Many different spices mixed to a paste give the lamb a very special aroma.

Chicken curry

MURG KARI

Famous dish

Serves 4
1 kg/2¼ lb chicken pieces
115 g/4 oz firm potatoes
2 tomatoes
2 cm/¾ inch piece fresh root ginger
2 fresh chillies
4 onions
4 garlic cloves
75 ml/5 tablespoons ghee
   (clarified butter) or vegetable oil
6 cm/2½ inch stick cinnamon bark
2 green cardamom pods
2 cloves
2 bay leaves
2.5 ml/½ teaspoon chilli powder
5 ml/1 teaspoon ground coriander
5 ml/1 teaspoon ground cumin
10 ml/2 teaspoons tomato paste
45 ml/3 tablespoons full-fat yogurt
salt
500 ml/17 fl oz water
10 ml/2 teaspoons garam masala

Approximately per portion:
1800 kj/430 kcal
36 g protein
26 g fat
10 g carbohydrate

● Approximate preparation
   time: 1 hour 10 minutes

---

1. Skin the chicken pieces and cut into portions. Cut the potatoes into 3 cm/1¼ inch cubes. Cut the tomatoes into quarters. Grate the ginger. Finely chop the chillies, onions and garlic.

2. Heat the ghee or oil over a medium heat. Fry the onions until well browned. Add the cinnamon, cardamom pods, cloves and bay leaves and fry for a further 2 minutes. Then add the chilli powder, coriander and cumin and fry for a further 2–3 minutes. Stir in the chillies, garlic and ginger. Add the tomatoes, chicken, tomato paste and yogurt and fry, stirring constantly, for about 5 minutes.

3. Add salt to taste and the water and bring to the boil. Simmer for 10 minutes, then add the potatoes. Cover and simmer over a low heat, stirring from time to time, for about 30 minutes. Sprinkle the garam masala over and serve hot.

Chicken in almond sauce

MURG MAN PASAND

Quick to make

Serves 6
1 kg/2¼ lb chicken breast fillets
6 onions
6 garlic cloves
3 cm/1¼ inch piece fresh root ginger
3 tomatoes
3 tablespoons ghee (clarified butter)
   or vegetable oil
4 cloves
4 x 5 cm/2 inch pieces
   cinnamon bark
6 green cardamom pods
7.5 ml/1½ teaspoons ground cumin
2.5 ml/½ teaspoon ground
   coriander
5 ml/1 teaspoon ground turmeric
1.5 ml/¼ teaspoon chilli powder
salt
45 ml/3 tablespoons ground,
   blanched almonds

250 ml/8 fl oz hot water
15 ml/1 tablespoon fresh coriander
   leaves and 15 ml/1 tablespoon
   blanched slivered almonds,
   to garnish

Approximately per portion:
1400 kj/330 kcal
40 g protein
16 g fat
4 g carbohydrate

● Approximate preparation
   time: 50 minutes

---

1. Skin the chicken breasts and cut into thin strips. Slice the onions. Crush the garlic. Grate the ginger. Dice the tomatoes.

2. Warm the ghee or oil in a karahi or large frying pan over a medium heat and fry the onions, stirring constantly, for about 10 minutes, until they are well browned. Add the garlic and ginger and cook for a further 2 minutes. Add the cloves, cinnamon and cardamom and cook for a further 2 minutes. Add the chicken and stir-fry for about 5 minutes. Stir in the cumin, ground coriander, turmeric and chilli powder and season to taste with salt.

3. Stir in the tomatoes, ground almonds and hot water. Bring to the boil, cover and simmer over a low heat, stirring frequently, for about 25 minutes. Transfer to a warm serving dish, garnish with the fresh coriander and slivered almonds and serve immediately.

Above: Chicken curry
Below: Chicken in almond sauce

Tandoori chicken

TANDOORI MURG

From northern India

A tandoor is a barrel-shaped clay oven that is heated with charcoal or wood. The red colour of the meat is traditional, but of course, you can do without it if you wish, as it has no effect on the taste.

Serves 4
1 kg/2¼ lb chicken pieces
   (legs and breast)
salt
150 ml/¼ pint vinegar
4 cm/1½ inch piece fresh root ginger
3 garlic cloves
300 ml/½ pint full-fat yogurt
2.5 ml/½ teaspoon chilli powder
10 ml/2 teaspoons sweet paprika
5 ml/1 teaspoon ground cumin
5 ml/1 teaspoon ground coriander
2.5 ml/½ teaspoon freshly ground
   black pepper
2.5 ml/½ teaspoon ground turmeric
5 ml/1 teaspoon ground nutmeg
1.5 ml/¼ teaspoon red
   food colouring

Approximately per portion:
860 kj/200 kcal
37 g protein
4 g fat
4 g carbohydrate

● Marinating time: 7–25 hours

● Approximate preparation
   time: 30 minutes

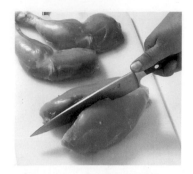

1. Skin the chicken pieces and cut the breast pieces in half. Using a sharp knife, make slashes in the meat so that the spices can penetrate well. Place the chicken pieces on a board and sprinkle with salt and vinegar. Leave to marinate for about 1 hour.

2. Grate the ginger and garlic and place in a large mixing bowl. Add the yogurt, chilli powder, paprika, cumin, coriander, black pepper, turmeric, nutmeg and food colouring and mix well. Put the chicken pieces into the yogurt mixture and turn to coat well. Cover and leave to marinate for 6–24 hours in the refrigerator.

3. Preheat the oven to 180°C/350°F/Gas 4 and line a baking sheet with foil. Remove the chicken pieces from the marinade and arrange them on the prepared baking sheet. Bake in the oven for about 45 minutes.

4. From time to time, baste the chicken pieces with the remaining marinade. Test with the point of a knife to see if the meat is cooked. When juices run clear, it is ready. Serve warm.

Seafood with coconut milk

JHINGA MALAI
Exquisite

Serves 4
500 g/1¼ lb cooked lobster or raw
    tiger prawns
4 onions
4 tablespoons ghee (clarified butter)
    or vegetable oil
5 ml/1 teaspoon garam masala
1 teaspoon ground turmeric
2.5 ml/½ teaspoon chilli powder
2 bay leaves
2 x 6 cm/2½ inch pieces
    cinnamon bark
2 green cardamom pods
2 cloves
400 ml/14 fl oz coconut milk
5 ml/1 teaspoon sugar
salt
Boiled basmati rice or Puri, to serve

Approximately per portion:
1300 kj/310 kcal
24 g protein
22 g fat
6 g carbohydrate

● Approximate preparation
   time: 1 hour

1. Remove the lobster meat from the shell or peel and devein the prawns. Finely chop 2 onions and purée the remaining onions in a food processor. Melt the ghee or heat the oil in a heavy-based frying pan over medium heat. Add the garam masala and cook for about 1 minute. Add the chopped onions and stir-fry until they are well browned.

2. Gradually stir in the puréed onions, turmeric, chilli powder, bay leaves, cinnamon bark, cardamom pods and cloves and stir-fry for about 5 minutes. If necessary, lower the heat.

3. Add half the coconut milk, sugar and salt to taste and mix well. Add the lobster or prawns to the sauce, turn carefully without breaking up the meat and cook over a low heat for about 10 minutes.

4. Stir in the remaining coconut milk and bring to the boil briefly. Serve with Boiled basmati rice (recipe on page 42) or Puri (recipe on page 44).

Fish curry

MACCHLI KARI

Exquisite

Serves 4
800 g/1¾ lb firm, fresh or frozen
    fish fillets, such as monkfish
2 tomatoes
2 potatoes
2 fresh chillies
4 cm/1½ inch piece fresh root ginger
15 ml/1 tablespoon mustard powder
250 ml/8 fl oz water
90 ml/6 tablespoons mustard oil
10 ml/2 teaspoons ground turmeric
10 ml/2 teaspoons ground cumin
10 ml/2 teaspoons sweet paprika
1.5 ml/¼ teaspoon chilli powder
60 ml/4 tablespoons full-fat yogurt
salt

Approximately per portion:
900 kj/210 kcal
16 g protein
14 g fat
6 g carbohydrate

● Approximate preparation
  time: 45 minutes

---

1. Cut the fish into bite-size
pieces. Cut the tomatoes into
quarters. Cut the potatoes into
sticks about 6 cm/2½ inches long
and 1 cm/½ inch wide. Seed and
finely chop the fresh chillies. Finely
chop the ginger. Mix together the
mustard powder and 90 ml/
5 tablespoons of the water to
make a thin, smooth paste and
set aside.

2. Heat the mustard oil in a large
frying pan. Add the fresh chillies,
ginger, turmeric, cumin, paprika
and chilli powder and cook over a
low heat, stirring constantly, for
about 5 minutes.

3. Add the yogurt and the
tomatoes and cook, stirring
constantly, for a further 5 minutes.
Add the remaining water and bring
to the boil, stirring.

4. Add the potatoes and the
prepared mustard, bring back to
the boil and cook for a further
5 minutes. Season with salt to
taste. Carefully add the fish pieces
to the pan, cover and cook over a
medium heat, stirring occasionally,
for 5 minutes. Serve immediately.

Fish in onion sauce

MACCHER KALIA

Good value

Serves 4
800 g/1¾ lb fresh salmon trout
    fillets
salt
7.5 ml/1½ teaspoons ground
    turmeric
3 onions
3 tomatoes
2 fresh chillies
4 cm/1½ inch piece fresh root ginger
2 garlic cloves
45 ml/3 tablespoons ghee
    (clarified butter)
2 bay leaves
2.5 ml/½ teaspoon cumin seeds
30 ml/2 tablespoons full-fat yogurt
150 ml/¼ pint water
10 ml/2 teaspoons mustard oil
5 ml/1 teaspoon garam masala
Boiled basmati rice, to serve

Approximately per portion:
1200 kj/290 kcal
23 g protein
18 g fat
5 g carbohydrate

● Approximate preparation
  time: 45 minutes

---

1. Cut the fish into pieces about
6 cm/2½ inches long. Sprinkle
2.5 ml/½ teaspoon of the salt and
2.5 ml/½ teaspoon of the turmeric
over the fish pieces and set aside.
Finely chop the onions. Cut the
tomatoes into quarters. Seed and
finely chop the chillies. Grate the
ginger and garlic.

2. Melt the ghee in a frying pan.
Add the bay leaves and cumin and
stir-fry over a medium heat for
about 1 minute. Add the onions
and stir-fry until they are well
browned. Stir in the ginger, garlic,
chillies and the remaining turmeric
and stir-fry for a further 2 minutes.
Add the tomatoes and yogurt. Mix
well and cook for 3 minutes. Add
the water and bring to the boil.

3. When the sauce begins to boil,
lower the heat, season with salt to
taste and carefully add the fish
pieces. Simmer over a low heat for
about 10 minutes.

4. Shortly before serving, sprinkle
the mustard oil and garam masala
over the fish. Turn the fish over
very carefully so that it does not
break. Serve hot with Boiled
basmati rice (recipe on page 42).

Above: Fish curry
Below: Fish in onion sauce

Boiled basmati rice

CHAWAL

Easy to make

Basmati rice is one of the oldest kinds of rice. Immigrants discovered it about 3,000 years ago in the highlands of Kashmir. This supreme rice grows at the foot of the Himalayas, where the melt water floods the plateau's terraced valleys. It is an aromatic rice. Hence the name basmati, which means 'fragrant rice'.

Serves 4
250 g/9 oz basmati rice
500 ml/17 fl oz water

Approximately per portion:
910 kj/220 kcal
5 g protein
1 g fat
46 g carbohydrate

● Approximate preparation time: 45 minutes

1. Put the rice in a sieve and rinse under cold running water. Transfer the rice to a bowl, add just enough water to cover and leave to soak for about 30 minutes.

2. Drain the rice and put it into a saucepan. Add the water and bring to the boil. Lower the heat. (If you are using an electric hotplate, turn it off.) Cover the pan and leave the rice to cook, without stirring, for about 15 minutes, until it is soft and has swelled up and absorbed all the liquid.

Vegetable pullao

PULLAO

For guests

Serves 4
400 g/14 oz basmati rice
8–10 saffron strands
45 ml/3 tablespoons boiling water
25 g/1 oz cashew nuts
90 ml/6 tablespoons ghee
  (clarified butter)
2 x 5 cm/2 inch pieces cinnamon
  bark
5 green cardamom pods
5 cloves
3 bay leaves
20 g/¾ oz currants
250 g/9 oz frozen mixed carrots
  and peas
25 g/1 oz blanched almonds,
  chopped
30 ml/2 tablespoons sugar
salt
1 litre/1¾ pints water

Approximately per portion:
3200 kj/760 kcal
12 g protein
38 g fat
92 g carbohydrate

● Approximate preparation time: 45 minutes

1. Put the rice in a sieve, wash in cold running water and leave to drain. Put the saffron strands in a small bowl and pour over the boiling water. Chop the cashew nuts finely.

2. Melt the ghee in a large saucepan over a medium heat. Add the cinnamon bark, cardamom, cloves and bay leaves and stir-fry for about 2 minutes.

3. Add the rice, currants and vegetables and stir-fry for 3 minutes. Then add the saffron together with its soaking liquid, almonds, cashew nuts, sugar and salt to taste and mix it all well together.

4. Pour in the water and bring to the boil. Lower the heat. (If you are using an electric hotplate, switch it off.) Cover the saucepan and cook the rice, without stirring, for about 15 minutes until it is soft and has swelled up and absorbed all the liquid.

Above: Boiled basmati rice
Below: Vegetable pullao

Chapatis

CHAPATI

Rather time-consuming

Chapati or ata flour is a special mixture of wheat flour and wholemeal, which you can buy in Asian shops.

Makes 16
400 g/14 oz chapati (ata) flour
30 ml/2 tablespoons ghee
  (clarified butter) or vegetable oil
200 ml/7 fl oz water
5 ml/1 teaspoon salt

Each chapati approximately:
410 kj/100 kcal
3 g protein
3 g fat
15 g carbohydrate

● Approximate preparation
  time: 1 hour

---

1. Put the flour, ghee or oil, water and the salt into a bowl.

2. Using your hands, mix to form a soft, smooth dough, adding a little more water if necessary. Turn the dough out on to a lightly floured surface and knead for at least 15 minutes. Form the dough into a ball, cover with a damp cloth and leave to stand for about 20 minutes.

3. Divide the dough into 16 pieces and shape these into small balls with the palms of your hands. Roll out each ball on a floured board to a thin circle. Make sure the chapatis are not bigger than the frying pan!

4. Preheat a frying pan for about 5 minutes over a medium heat. Fry 1 chapati for about 1 minute, turn and fry the other side for 1 further minute, until golden.

5. Wrap the cooked chapati in aluminium foil to keep warm. Cook the remaining chapatis in the same way. It is best to cook them shortly before serving.

Puris

PURI

Exquisite • For guests

It is pleasant to watch the flat circles of dough frying in the hot oil and puffing up like balloons.

Makes 15
150 g/5 oz wholemeal flour
2.5 ml/½ teaspoon salt
30 ml/2 tablespoons ghee
  (clarified butter) or vegetable oil
75 ml/5 tablespoons water
vegetable oil, for deep-frying

Approximately per puri:
480 kj/110 kcal
1 g protein
10 g fat
6 g carbohydrate

● Approximate preparation
  time: 45 minutes

---

1. Put the flour, salt and ghee or oil into a bowl. Slowly add the water and knead the mixture by hand for about 10 minutes, until it forms a smooth, elastic dough.

2. Divide the dough into 15 equal-sized balls. Press the balls flat and roll each out on an oiled surface into a flat circle about 15 cm/ 6 inches in diameter. Do not stack the puris on top of each other, as they will stick together.

3. Heat the oil to a high temperature in a karahi or frying pan. When the oil begins to smoke, reduce the heat.

4. Lower 1 dough circle into the oil. Gently pat down the middle of the puri with a perforated spoon, until it puffs up like a balloon. Turn over and fry the other side until it turns golden brown. Remove the puri from the pan and drain on kitchen paper. Keep warm while you cook the remaining puris in the same way. Serve hot.

Above: Chapatis
Below: Puris

Paratha

PARATHA
Rather time-consuming

Parathas are rather like chapatis, but are flakier and softer. They take longer to prepare, but their rich taste is well worth the extra effort.

Makes 16
400g/14 oz chapati (ata) flour, plus
*   extra for dusting*
30 ml/2 tablespoons ghee
*   (clarified butter) or vegetable oil*
250 ml/8 fl oz water
5 ml/1 teaspoon salt
melted ghee, for brushing

Approximately per piece:
510 kj/120 kcal
3 g protein
6 g fat
15 g carbohydrate

● Approximate preparation
time: 1½ hours

---

1. Put the flour, ghee or oil, water and salt into a bowl.

2. Mix by hand to form a soft, smooth dough, adding a little more water if necessary. Turn out the dough and knead for at least 15 minutes. Form the dough into a ball, brush with melted ghee and leave to stand for about 20 minutes.

3. Divide the dough into 16 pieces and shape these into small balls with the palms of your hands. Roll out each ball on a floured board to a flat circle about 17 cm/

6½ inches in diameter. Brush the surface with a little melted ghee and fold in half, then fold in half again. Dust with flour and roll out again to form a triangle with sides that are 20 cm/8 inches long.

4. Preheat a chapati pan or a heavy-based frying pan over a medium heat. Brush the pan with a little melted ghee. Place 1 paratha in the pan and fry for about 1 minute over a medium heat. Brush the upper surface with melted ghee, turn over and fry the other side for about 1 minute. Turn over again and fry for a further 1 minute. The paratha is ready when it is golden brown on both sides. Keep warm wrapped in foil while you cook the remaining parathas in the same way.

Naan

NAAN
For guests

Naan is the famous Mogul bread that was originally baked in a tandoor oven. However, using a conventional oven still provides the authentic flavour.

Makes 9
about 150 ml/¼ pint milk
10 ml/2 teaspoons sugar
15 g/½ oz fresh yeast
500 g/1¼ lb flour
salt
5 ml/1 teaspoon baking powder
30 ml/2 tablespoons vegetable oil,
*   plus extra for greasing*
150 ml/¼ pint full-fat yogurt
1 egg, lightly beaten

Approximately per piece:
1065 kj/220 kcal
6 g protein
5 g fat
47 g carbohydrate

● Approximate preparation
time: 1½ hours

● Resting time: about 1¼ hours

---

1. Warm the milk until it is tepid. Put 5 ml/1 teaspoon of the sugar, the yeast and the milk into a bowl and stir well. Cover and leave to stand for about 15 minutes.

2. Sift the flour into a large bowl. Stir in 2.5 ml/½ teaspoon salt and the baking powder. Gradually stir in the remaining sugar, the milk and yeast mixture, the oil, yogurt and beaten egg. Knead the dough well. Leave to rest in a warm place for about 1 hour.

3. Preheat the oven to 220°C/ 425°F/Gas 7 and grease a baking sheet with oil. Knead the dough again and form into 6 balls with the palms of your hands. Roll out the first ball on a floured surface to a tear shape (about 1 cm/ ½ inch thick, 25 cm/10 inches long and 13 cm/5 inches wide).

4. Place the naan on the prepared baking sheet and immediately put this into the middle of the hot oven. Bake for about 8 minutes. Wrap the baked naan in a napkin and keep warm. Cook the remainder in the same way.

Above: Paratha
Below: Naan

Fried flat bread with peas

KOTSCHURI

Easy to make

Makes 16
200 g/7 oz flour
60 ml/4 tablespoons ghee
*   (clarified butter) or vegetable oil*
salt
120 ml/4 fl oz water
150 g/5 oz frozen peas, thawed
5 ml/1 teaspoon garam masala
2.5 ml/½ teaspoon ground cumin
vegetable oil, for deep-frying

Approximately per piece:
750 kj/180 kcal
2 g protein
14 g fat
11 g carbohydrate

● Approximate preparation
  time: 1 hour

1. First make the dough. Put the flour, 30 ml/2 tablespoons ghee or oil and 2.5 ml/½ teaspoon salt into a bowl and mix well. Add the water and knead the mixture for about 15 minutes, until the dough is soft and elastic. Cover with a damp cloth and leave to stand for about 20 minutes.

2. Meanwhile purée the peas in a food processor. Warm the rest of the ghee or oil in a frying pan over a medium heat.

3. Add the puréed peas and stir-fry over a low heat for about 3 minutes. Stir in the garam masala, cumin and salt to taste and set aside to cool.

4. Mix the dough with the cooled pea purée. If it becomes too soft, add more flour and knead well.

5. Divide the dough into 16 large, equal-size balls. Press each one flat and roll it out on an oiled work surface to a circle about 15 cm/ 6 inches in diameter.

Variation
The bread also tastes good if you use potatoes instead of peas. Dice 3 medium floury potatoes and boil in lightly salted water until soft. Strain and mash while hot. Continue the recipe as for the peas.

6. Heat the vegetable oil in a karahi or deep-fryer. It is hot enough when you can dip a wooden spoon into it and no bubbles rise.

7. Place 1 dough circle in the hot oil. Gently pat it down with a perforated spoon until the bread puffs up like a balloon.

8. Turn the bread over and fry the other side until golden brown. Remove the bread from the pan and drain on kitchen paper. Keep warm while you fry the remaining bread in the same way. Serve warm.

Aubergine raita

BAIGAN-KA-RAITA

Exquisite

Serves 6
500 g/1¼ lb aubergines
1 firm tomato
1 fresh chilli
1 onion
30 ml/2 tablespoons vegetable oil
10 ml/2 teaspoons garam masala
salt
250 ml/8 fl oz full-fat yogurt

Approximately per portion:
330 kj/80 kcal
3 g protein
5 g fat
5 g carbohydrate

● Approximate preparation
time: 1 hour

1. Preheat the oven to 200°C/ 400°F/Gas 6. Slash the skins of the aubergines, arrange them on a baking sheet and bake in the middle of the oven, turning them frequently, until they are soft.

2. Remove the aubergines and peel off their skins. Finely chop the flesh.

3. Dice the tomato. Seed and finely chop the chilli. Finely chop the onion. Heat the oil in a frying pan over a medium heat. Fry the onion and chilli.

4. Add the tomato, garam masala and salt to the pan and stir-fry for about 1 minute. Add the aubergines and mix well. Fry for a further 3 minutes, then remove from the heat.

5. Put the yogurt into a bowl and stir in the contents of the frying pan. Mix thoroughly and allow to cool. Store in the refrigerator until ready for serving.

Cucumber and tomato raita

KHEERA-TAMATAR-RAITA

Quick to make

Raitas are served with all dishes in India. Use only naturally fermented, full-fat yogurt.

Serves 6
1 cucumber
2 firm tomatoes
1 medium onion
300 ml/½ pint full-fat yogurt
5 ml/1 teaspoon ground cumin
salt
15 ml/1 tablespoon vegetable oil
5 ml/1 teaspoon black
mustard seeds

Approximately per portion:
240 kj/66 kcal
2 g protein
4 g fat
4 g carbohydrate

● Approximate preparation
time: 20 minutes

1. Peel and dice the cucumber. Dice the tomato and finely chop the onion.

2. Put the yogurt into a bowl. Add the cucumber, tomato, onion and cumin and season to taste with salt. Mix well.

3. Heat the oil and quickly fry the mustard seeds in it. Add them to the yogurt mixture and mix carefully. Chill until ready to serve.

Mint sauce

DAHI POODINA

Quick to make

Serves 6
50 g/2 oz fresh mint or 30 ml/
2 tablespoons bottled mint
200 ml/7 fl oz full-fat yogurt
salt
2.5 ml/½ teaspoon ground cumin
1.5 ml/¼ teaspoon ground chilli

Approximately per portion:
110 kj/25 kcal
2 g protein
1 g fat
1 g carbohydrate

● Approximate preparation
time: 10 minutes

1. Wash the fresh mint and chop finely. Stir it together with all the other ingredients and then chill until ready to serve.

Above: Aubergine raita
Centre: Cucumber and tomato raita
Below: Mint sauce

Apple chutney

SEB-KI-CHATNI

Good to prepare in advance

Serves 10
1 kg/2¼ lb tart apples
2 fresh chillies
45 ml/3 tablespoons ghee
    (clarified butter)
10 ml/2 teaspoons five-spice
    mixture (panch foron)
5 ml/1 teaspoon ground turmeric
5 ml/1 teaspoon ground cumin
salt
150 ml/¼ pint water
45 ml/3 tablespoons muscovado
    sugar
30 ml/2 tablespoons lemon juice

Approximately per portion:
500 kj/120 kcal
0.3 g protein
6 g fat
16 g carbohydrate

● Approximate preparation
    time: 45 minutes

---

1. Peel, core and chop the apples. Seed and halve the chillies.

2. Melt the ghee. Add the chillies, five-spice mixture, turmeric and cumin and season to taste with salt. Stir-fry over a medium heat for about 30 seconds. Add the apples and stir-fry for a further 4 minutes. Add the water, cover and cook over a low heat for about 20 minutes, until the apples are soft.

3. Stir in the sugar and lemon juice and cook over a medium heat, stirring frequently, until thickened. Remove from the heat and set aside to cool.

Mango chutney

AM CHATNI

Easy to make

Chutneys are served in small portions with Indian dishes. They can be sour, hot, sweet or spicy and stimulate the appetite.

Serves 6
1 large mango
2 fresh chillies
10 ml/2 teaspoons cornflour
280 ml/9 fl oz water
1.5 ml/¼ teaspoon ground turmeric
salt
115 g/4 oz muscovado sugar
15 ml/1 tablespoon ghee
    (clarified butter) or vegetable oil
5 ml/1 teaspoon black mustard
    seeds
2 dried chillies
pinch of asafoetida (optional)

Approximately per portion:
520 kj/120 kcal
0 g protein
4 g fat
23 g carbohydrate

● Approximate preparation
    time: 50 minutes

---

1. Peel the mango and cut the flesh away from the stone in slices about 5 mm/¼ inch thick. Seed and finely chop the fresh chillies. Stir together the cornflour and 30 ml/2 tablespoons of the water and set aside.

2. Bring the remaining water to the boil in a saucepan and add the turmeric and salt to taste. Add the

mango slices with the fresh chillies. Simmer over a medium heat for about 20 minutes, until the mango slices are soft. Increase the heat and boil the chutney for about a further 5 minutes. Stir in the sugar and cornflour paste and bring to the boil again. Remove the pan from the heat.

3. Heat the ghee or oil in a small saucepan. Add the mustard seeds and the dried chillies and stir-fry briefly. Stir in the asafoetida, if using, and add the contents of the pan to the chutney. Mix well together and set aside to cool. When it cools, the chutney will become a bit thicker.

Tip

You can ladle the cooked chutney into a glass jar and store for up to two weeks in a cool place or in the refrigerator. Use a screw-top jar with a non-metallic lid.

Above: Mango chutney
Below: Apple chutney

Coconut chutney

NARIYAL-CHATNI

Easy to make • Exquisite

Serves 4
200 g/7 oz grated coconut
120 ml/4 fl oz water
45 ml/3 tablespoons lemon juice
1 onion
6 cm/2½ inch piece fresh root ginger
1 fresh chilli
30 ml/2 tablespoons vegetable oil
15 ml/1 tablespoon black
  mustard seeds
15 ml/1 tablespoon urid dhal
salt

Approximately per portion:
1200 kj/290 kcal
2 g protein
14 g fat
39 g carbohydrate

● Approximate preparation
  time: 30 minutes

---

1. Put the grated coconut, water and lemon juice into a food processor and work to make a smooth purée.

2. Finely chop the onion. Grate the ginger. Seed and finely chop the chilli. Add the onion, chilli and ginger to the coconut purée and work again briefly.

3. Heat the oil in a frying pan over medium heat. Add the mustard seeds and fry for about 30 seconds. Add the urid dhal and stir-fry for about 1 minute. Add the coconut purée to the pan. Mix together well and stir-fry for a

further 2 minutes, but be careful not to allow the coconut to brown. Season the chutney with salt and set aside to cool.

Tip

When buying a fresh coconut, choose one that is heavy for its size. Hold it close to your ear and give it a good shake. If it is full of milk, it is likely to be quite fresh. If it has dried out, the flesh is likely to be rancid. It is also worth checking the 'eyes' for mould. To crack the nut, first pierce two of the 'eyes' and drain off the milk, then enclose the nut in a plastic bag and hit it with a hammer.

Tomato chutney

TAMATAR-CHATNI

Serves 4
5 ripe tomatoes
  (about 300 g/11 oz)
3 cm/1¼ inch piece fresh root ginger
115 g/4 oz currants
75 ml/5 tablespoons sugar
120 ml/4 fl oz water
2.5 ml/½ teaspoon ground turmeric
salt
10 ml/2 teaspoons ghee
  (clarified butter)
5 ml/1 teaspoon five-spice mixture
  (panch foron)
5 ml/1 teaspoon fennel seeds
5 ml/1 teaspoon cumin seeds
juice of ½ lemon

Approximately per portion:
740 kj/180 kcal
1 g protein
3 g fat
37 g carbohydrate

● Approximate preparation
  time: 40 minutes

---

1. Cut the tomatoes into quarters. Grate the ginger. Put the tomatoes, currants and ginger into a saucepan. Add the sugar and water. Bring to the boil and cook for about 20 minutes over a low heat, until the mixture thickens. Add the turmeric and salt to taste, cover and boil for a further 5 minutes.

2. Melt the ghee in a small saucepan over a medium heat. Add the five-spice mixture, stir-fry briefly, then pour over the tomatoes. Mix well.

3. In another pan, dry-fry the fennel and cumin seeds over a medium heat until they give off their aroma and are lightly coloured. Stir the seeds into the tomato mixture.

4. Stir in the lemon juice. Remove the chutney from the heat and set aside to cool.

Above: Coconut chutney.
Below: Tomato chutney.

Mango dessert

MALAI AM

Easy to make • Quick

Serves 4–6
300 ml/½ pint double cream
10 ml/2 teaspoons sugar
400 g/14 oz can mango pulp

For 6 people approximately per portion:
730 kj/170 kcal
1 g protein
11 g fat
18 g carbohydrate

● Approximate preparation time: 10 minutes

1. Beat together the 200 ml/7 fl oz cream and the sugar. Fold in the mango pulp.

2. Spoon the dessert into individual dishes and chill until ready to serve. Beat the remaining cream until thick and use to decorate the desserts.

Vermicelli in cream sauce

SEMIAN

Serves 6
1.5 litres/2½ pints milk
15 ml/1 tablespoon butter
6 cloves
1 teaspoon ground cardamom
130 g/4½ oz Indian vermicelli
115 g/4 oz sugar
15 ml/1 tablespoon finely ground pistachio nuts
15 ml/1 tablespoon finely ground almonds

200 ml/7 fl oz double cream
5 ml/1 teaspoon rose water

Approximately per portion:
2300 kj/550 kcal
13 g protein
36 g fat
45 g carbohydrate

● Approximate preparation time: 40 minutes

1. Bring the milk to the boil, lower the heat and simmer. Meanwhile, melt the butter in a large saucepan. Add the cloves and 2.5 ml/½ teaspoon of the cardamom and stir-fry briefly. Break the vermicelli into pieces, add to the pan and stir-fry until golden brown.

2. Pour in the milk, bring to the boil and cook over a medium heat for about 5 minutes. Stir in the sugar, pistachio nuts and almonds. Lower the heat and simmer the mixture for a further 15 minutes until thickened.

3. Remove the saucepan from the heat. Add the cream and rose water. Transfer the vermicelli to a serving dish and decorate with the remaining cardamom. Serve warm or cold.

Carrot halva

GAJAR HALVA

Serves 4
400 g/14 oz carrots
75 ml/5 tablespoons ghee (clarified butter)
30 ml/2 tablespoons chopped almonds

30 ml/2 tablespoons semolina
300 ml/½ pint milk
45 ml/3 tablespoons sugar
30 ml/2 tablespoons currants
5 ml/1 teaspoon ground cardamom

Approximately per portion:
2100 kj/500 kcal
5 g protein
40 g fat
28 g carbohydrate

● Approximate preparation time: 50 minutes

● Approximate cooling time: 1 hour

1. Grate the carrots. Melt 45 ml/3 tablespoons of the ghee in a saucepan over a medium heat. Add the grated carrots and cook over a low heat, stirring frequently, for about 20 minutes.

2. Melt the remaining ghee in a small pan. Add the almonds and the semolina and stir-fry for about 5 minutes. Remove from the heat and set aside.

3. Put the milk, sugar and currants in a large saucepan and bring to the boil. Add the carrots and the almond and semolina paste and cook over a medium heat, stirring constantly, for a further 15 minutes, until the halva has thickened. Finally, stir in the ground cardamom.

4. Transfer the halva to a serving plate, leave to cool for about 1 hour, then cut into strips.

Above: Mango dessert
Centre: Carrot halva
Below: Vermicelli in cream sauce

Sweetmeats in syrup

GULAB JAMUN

Unusual

Makes 40 (Serves 8–10)
1 litre/1¾ pints water
750 g/1 lb 10 oz sugar
15 ml/1 tablespoon rose water
120 ml/4 fl oz milk
175 g/6 oz milk powder
45 g/1¾ oz flour
5 ml/1 teaspoon baking powder
5 ml/1 teaspoon ground cardamom
15 ml/1 tablespoon ghee
  (clarified butter)
vegetable oil, for deep-frying

**For 10 people
approximately per portion:**
1700 kj/405 kcal
1 g protein
10 g fat
80 g carbohydrate

● Approximate preparation
  time: 1 hour

---

1. Heat the water in a saucepan
with the sugar and boil for about
5 minutes, until the sugar has
dissolved. Stir in the rose water,
remove from the heat, pour into a
serving dish and set aside.

2. Warm the milk. Mix together
the milk powder, flour, baking
powder, cardamom and ghee in a
bowl with your fingertips. Slowly
pour in the warm milk. Mix all the
ingredients well until the dough is
firm and workable. It should be
soft enough almost to stick to your
hands. If it is too dry, gradually mix
in a little more milk.

3. Shape the dough into little balls
about 2 cm/¾ inch in diameter.

4. Heat the oil in a karahi or
saucepan over a low heat. Do not
allow it to become too hot. Add
the dough balls, in batches if
necessary, and fry, turning
frequently, for about 15 minutes,
until they are evenly browned.

5. To test whether the sweetmeats
are cooked, place 1 in the syrup.
If it does not fall apart after
2 minutes, it is cooked. Drain the
sweetmeats well on kitchen paper
and then toss them gently in the
syrup. Serve warm or cold in the
syrup. You can keep gulab jamuns
for a few days, in a covered
container in the refrigerator.

Moong dhal sweetmeats

MOONG LADDU

Makes 20–25 (Serves 8–10)
500 g/1¼ lb moong dhal
375 g/12 oz ghee (clarified butter)
375 g/12 oz icing sugar
5 ml/1 teaspoon ground cardamom

**For 10 people
approximately per portion:**
3000 kj/710 kcal
19 g protein
49 g fat
49 g carbohydrate

● Approximate preparation
  time: 1½ hours

● Approximate cooling time:
  1 hour

---

1. Grind the moong dhal to a fine
flour. Put the flour into a heavy-
based pan and cook over a low
heat, stirring constantly, for about
1 hour, until it turns golden.
Remove from the heat and set
aside to cool.

2. Melt the ghee in a saucepan, but
do not allow it to get very hot.
Add the icing sugar, remove from
the heat and mix well together
with your hands.

3. Add the cooled flour and
cardamom to the ghee and sugar
paste and mix well. If the paste is
too soft to be workable, chill
briefly in the refrigerator.

4. Shape the mixture into 20–25
walnut-sized balls and set aside for
1 hour to cool.

Tip

The sweetmeats can be kept
for up to 4 weeks in the
refrigerator.

Above: Sweetmeats in syrup
Below: Moong dhal sweetmeats

Sweet lassi

MITHI LASSI

Easy to make

Serves 4
500 ml/17 fl oz full-fat yogurt
250 ml/8 fl oz ice-cold water
60 ml/4 tablespoons sugar
ice cubes (optional)

> **Approximately per portion:**
> 530 kj/130 kcal
> 4 g protein
> 4 g fat
> 18 g carbohydrate
>
> ● Approximate preparation
>   time: 10 minutes

1. Beat together the yogurt, water and sugar with a whisk or in an electric blender until it becomes frothy.

2. Pour into glasses, add the ice cubes, if using, and serve.

Savoury lassi

NAMKIN LASSI

Quick • Exquisite

Serves 4
500 ml/17 fl oz full-fat yogurt
250 ml/8 fl oz ice-cold water
5 ml/1 teaspoon salt
15 g/½ oz fresh mint,
    finely chopped
5 ml/1 teaspoon lemon juice
ice cubes (optional)
mint sprigs, to decorate

> **Approximately per portion:**
> 320 kj/75 kcal
> 4 g protein
> 4 g fat
> 5 g carbohydrate
>
> ● Approximate preparation
>   time: 10 minutes

1. Beat together the yogurt, water, salt, chopped mint and lemon juice with a whisk or in an electric blender until it becomes frothy.

2. Pour into glasses, add the ice cubes, if using, and decorate with mint sprigs.

Variation
Instead of mint, you can use 2.5 ml/½ teaspoon ground cumin. Beat a pinch with the yogurt, water and salt and use the remainder to sprinkle over the drinks.

Spiced tea

MASALA CHAI

For guests

Serves 4
5 cm/2 inch cinnamon stick
6 green cardamom pods
6 cloves
500 ml/17 fl oz water
500 ml/17 fl oz milk
sugar or honey to taste
75 ml/5 teaspoons black tea

> **Approximately per portion:**
> 500 kj/120 kcal
> 4 g protein
> 4 g fat
> 16 g carbohydrate
>
> ● Approximate preparation
>   time: 20 minutes

1. Dry-fry the cinnamon, cardamom and cloves in a frying pan, stirring constantly.

2. Put the water into a saucepan with the fried spices and bring to the boil. Cover and simmer over a low heat for about 10 minutes.

3. Add milk and sugar or honey to taste and bring back to the boil. Remove the saucepan from the heat and add the tea. Cover and leave to infuse for 3–5 minutes. Strain into cups and serve.

Variation
Spiced coffee is also a favourite in India. Bring 1 litre/1¾ pints water and milk to the boil. Add 50 ml/ 10 teaspoons finely ground coffee, 4 green cardamom pods and about 90 ml/6 teaspoons sugar and simmer for 3 minutes. Strain and serve hot.

Tip

It is advisable to use a strong Assam or Nilgiri tea to make the spicy tea. When it combines with the milk, it turns a beautiful brown colour.

Above: Sweet lassi
Centre: Savoury lassi
Below: Spiced tea

Great Little Cook Books
Indian Cooking

Published originally under the title
Indisch kochen by Gräfe und Unzer
Verlag GmbH, München

© 1994 by Gräfe und Unzer Verlag
GmbH, München

English-language edition
© 1998 by Transedition Limited,
Oxford, England

This edition published by
Aura Books plc

Translation:
Translate-A-Book, Oxford

Editing:
Linda Doeser

Typesetting:
Organ Graphic, Abingdon

10 9 8 7 6 5 4 3 2 1
Printed in Dubai

ISBN 1 901683 21 4

Note:
Quantities for all recipes are given
in both metric and imperial
measures and, if appropriate, in
standard measuring spoons. They
are not interchangeable, so readers
should follow one set or the other.
5 ml = 1 teaspoon
15 ml = 1 tablespoon

Bikash and Marcela Kumar
live in Munich with their two
children. They have been running
courses in Indian cookery in
various colleges for the last ten
years. Bikash Kumar was born in
Calcutta and has lived in Germany
since 1973. Besides his family and
professional occupations, he
devotes his time to spreading the
knowledge of Indian history,
culture and customs among
Germans. Marcela Kumar's love of
Indian cooking began with her
marriage. Countless visits to India
kept increasing it. The couple have
a shop for Indian spices, groceries
and specialities in Munich.

Odette Teubner
was taught her craft by her father,
the internationally renowned food
photographer, Christian Teubner.
At present she works exclusively in
the Teubner Studio for Food
Photography. In her spare time she
is an enthusiastic painter of
children's portraits. She uses her
own son as a model.

Dorothee Gödert
After finishing her studies in
photography, she started work as a
photographer of still-lifes and
interiors. After her visit to
Princeton in the United States she
specialized in food photography.
She has worked with a number of
well-known food photographers
and, since April 1988, she has been
working in the Teubner Studio.